From The Beaches To The Baltic: The Story Of The 7th Armored Division

United States Army

FROM THE BEACHES TO THE BALTIC

THE STORY OF THE
7TH ARMORED DIVISION

This is the story of a fighting outfit, the 7th Armored Division. No words can adequately describe its exploits nor can a book of this size do more than highlight the division's combat history. From the shores of the English Channel to the waters of the Baltic Sea, the division blazed a path marked by achievements concerning which volumes could be written. This account has been compiled for the men whose heroism, devotion to duty and blood made those achievements possible. It is a story which will forever be enshrined in the hearts of those staunch fighting men who composed the 7th Armored.

Robert W. Hasbrouck

MAJOR GENERAL, U. S. ARMY
COMMANDING

FROM THE BEACHES
TO THE BALTIC

(The Story of the 7th Armored Division)

What follows is loosely called the "story of the 7th Armored Division". It isn't a complete story, for no story involving fighting men could possibly be truly complete without the stories of each of those men. This, rather, is a brief of the things that were done by a fighting command - how it whipped the best that the German High Command could muster, and fought on its own two legs from the beaches of Normandy to the sandy shores of the Baltic Sea on the north coastline of Germany.

The 7th Armored Division was activated March 1, 1942, at Camp Polk, Louisiana, under the command of Brigadier General L. McD. Silvester. (Shortly thereafter promoted to the rank of Major General). At Camp Polk it sweated through training and maneuvers in '42, and grew into a fighting team. It sort of annexed the name "Lucky" at Camp Polk, and was referred to as "The Lucky 7th" when it moved to California for desert training. Here it stayed in and around Camp

Coxcomb for five months, learning and perspiring — becoming a fighting outfit. The Division went back to the South, arriving at Fort Benning, Georgia in August, 1943, where it remained until mid- April, 1944, when it staged at Camp Myles Standish, Mass. A week there, and then the 7th went to Camp Shanks, N. Y., where it stayed until June 6, D-day in Europe. On that day, the men of the Division boarded the Queen Mary in New York harbor. Debarkation was at Greenock, Scotland on June 13. Then came Tidworth Barracks, Wiltshire, England, where final preparations were made for entering combat. The call came, and on August 7th, the 7th Armored Division rolled to the ports of Southampton and Portsmouth, boarded LCT's and Liberty ships to cross the English Channel. The first boatloads of 7th Armored Division men and equipment put foot on French soil on August 10, 1944.

From aboard a Liberty ship on the English Channel, men of the 7th Armored gaze expectantly for the French shoreline.

4

COMBAT! The Fight Across France ο

From August 10 to August 14, units of the Division debarked at both Omaha and Utah beaches and assembled near La Haye du Puits, France. While some of its troops were still at anchor off the beaches of Normandy, other troops of the Division were engaged in bitter initial combat 190 miles to the east, spearheading XX Corps, Third US Army, in the breakthrough operations from the costly beachhead.

In spite of a rousing welcome by a jubilant French population, and immaterial aid in the form of kisses and cognac, there was fighting — bitter fighting — and men died! There was no major action until troops reached. Chartres; that is, there was no action big enough for the folks back home to read about in the headlines, but there was blood spilled, and it was American blood, and 7th Armored Division's blood at that. Every fight has its major actions and the 7th had a lion's share of them.

Chartres, a vital road center and famous cathedral city of France, populated by 23,000 then frenzied citizens, was important to the Germans. They augmented the thousand man garrison with 2,000 stragglers; it looked as if Jerry was dead set on holding the city. On August 16, the Division attacked. CC"A", under Col. Dwight A. Rosebaum, struck eastward on a route to the North of the bastion; Brig. Gen. John B. Thompson's CC"B" smashed into the city.

A task force under Lt. Col. Leslie Allison, 23rd Armored Infantry Battalion, entered the city from the west, and battled fiercely through the 16th and 17th in clearing the enemy from the northern part of Chartres. Another task force, commanded by Lt. Col. Robert C. Erlenbusch, 31st Tank Battalion, aided the attack from the southwest, running into bitter resistance in the vicinity of the railroad station in the southern part of the city; this resistance was completely crushed by sheer guts and plenty of firepower by August 18.

An important and well-defended airfield east of Chartres had meanwhile been attacked by the 38th Armored Infantry Battalion and the 31st Tank Battalion, and after a brief but bitter fight, the remains of the enemy force withdrew to the east. CC"B" moved to the north to join the other forces of the Division near Dreux. Liberated Chartres, with the magnificent cathedral spared the ravages of modern weaponry, first prize for the 7th Armored Division paid for with a battle's sweat and blood, was turned over to the 5th Infantry Division.

There was no heavy fighting (as the Division came to know it) at Dreux. There was German artillery, and there was infiltration, and even the enemy's air force struck at the Division. While the radios yammered that the Germans were on the run, and hometown

Troops of the Division enter a war-torn French town.

6

newspapers told of the greatest victory of all time, the men and machines of the 7th Armored faced a hard-fighting enemy — and were ordered to hold this city.

The Division was ordered to move to the east on August 20th to establish crossings over the Seine River. Two columns were directed at Melun, Seine river town some 40 miles south of Paris, and these forces plowed through enemy troops, battering down all resistance, churning on towards Melun. By mid-afternoon on August 22, elements of CC "R" were fighting a determined enemy in the outskirts of that town. CC"A" to the north, had reached Pont Thierry, a village north of Melun.

And then men of the 48th Armored Infantry Battalion, commanded by Lt. Col. Richard Chappuis, crossed the Seine at Tilly, two miles north of Pont Thierry. Distinction was theirs! Troops of the 7th Armored Division were *the first Allied soldiers to cross the Seine River in this war.* It was not an easy crossing. As the men crossed the river, 88mm shells splashed water over the gunwales of their assault boats, and mortar projectiles fell like rain. Supporting fires kept the Germans in their holes; consequently the 7th suffered very few casualties on the crossing. But those men did the job; all of them reached the opposite shores and moved on. They routed the enemy — slaughtered the opposing forces, and seized and held a bridgehead. Then they developed it so that on the following day, Company A, 33rd Armored Engineer Battalion, assisted by a Treadway Bridge Company, succeeded in thrusting a bridge across the bloody Seine. It was the first bridge that the Allies put across that stream, and it was no more a pleasant task than any doughboy's assault crossing. The job was completed during the morning hours of August 24 while German shells roared into the bridgesite area like express trains. As CC"A" pushed onward from the bridgehead, a companion force that had crossed the newly-built bridge attacked the enemy forces that still held on in Melun. This French city must have been declared vital to the effort of the German defenders, for the defense around it became more and more rugged with the passing of each hour. The troops of the Division, led by the 23rd Armored Infantry Battalion, ran into minefields and dug-in enemy, and that enemy fought back. Mortar and artillery fire was heavy, and the troops attacking the town didn't race into the populated areas. The enemy's

Troops of the 7th Armored Division cross the SEINE River at TILLY, France.

effort to establish a main defensive line on the Seine River was overcome, however, and Melun was completely occupied on August 25.

With the capture of Melun and the establishment of the bridgehead over the Seine, the enemy's water barrier was broken — ripped asunder by a determined force directed in a smashing attack. The German defenders were killed in great numbers, and others were pressed rearward to Division prisoner of war cages; much material and many supplies were captured in Melun, as was "Radio Paris", the most powerful Nazi radio outlet in Europe which was taken intact. "Radio Paris", primary note in Hitler's daily song to the oppressed peoples of the Continent, was relieved as Nazidom's servant.

It is said that good warriors never rest. Whether by lot or by choice, this adage was fast being proven quite true for the troops of the 7th Armored.

Now that the Seine River had been crossed, the Division was directed to the northward, towards another river — the Marne, upon whose banks nestled the city of Chateau-Thierry; famous from World War I as a scene of fighting against the German hordes, and north of which lay Reims, famous for its cathedral and its vast champagne industry. Towards these objectives the men and machines of the 7th Armored poured, in hot, bitter pursuit of desperate enemy forces.

On August 27, CC"A", in three columns, moved on Chateau-Thierry. Each column had tanks, tank destroyers, artillery, infantry and engineers. To CC" A" 's right, or east, the forces of CC"B" likewise attacked to establish bridgeheads over the Marne to the east of

Chateau-Thierry. CC"B" moved behind the reconnaissance screen of Lt. Col. Vincent Boylan's 87th Cav Rcn Sqdn (Mecz), fighting fact-finders of the Division.

As CC"A" moved on Chateau-Thierry, it encountered savage bands of enemy troops, desperate in their efforts to hold off the attackers, desperate to save their own lines. Relentless pressure was maintained; CC"A" moved ahead. Bitter battles, fought and won at La Ferte Gaucher and Montmirail yielded prisoners and equipment, and the inevitable dead and wounded enemy. Gasoline had become critical for all forces. The speed of the attack was breathtaking, and supplies were simply being outrun. On Monday, August 25, Lt. Col. Edward T. McConnell's task force drained all available Jerry cans into hungry machines, and struck out on CC"A"'s extreme left flank, on the direct route to Chateau-Thierry. The task force smashed bodily through formidable road blocks south of the city, and under withering artillery fire, pursued a desperate, clinging enemy into Chateau-Thierry. Pressure was maintained, and within this famous city of battle, the tanks and guns of the 7th Armored smashed what enemy there was south of the Marne and pushed on to capture the main bridge over the river. The speed of the attack had simply enabled the troops to catch and annihilate all the enemy before they could establish a proposed line on the stream.

Meanwhile, the right hand force of the Division (CC"B") took Provins, to the east of Melun, and pressed on northward. After cutting a bewildered, retreating enemy force to ribbons, this force, too, reached the Marne — at Epernay. The 23rd Armored Infantry Battalion smashed into defenses on the outskirts of Epernay, and

10

through them. The infantrymen reached the river, only to find the bridge destroyed, and they, and the armor that followed, were subjected to merciless antitank, mortar, and artillery fire, from the high ground to the north of the city, where the enemy had used his time to site his weapons.

The command was delayed, but not halted. In night operations on August 28 and 29, the 33rd Armored Engineer Battalion, aided by the 135th Combat Engineer Battalion, laid two bridges across the Marne. The enemy fires had been largely neutralized by the accurate shooting of elements of the Division's artillery, and CC"B" crossed the Marne in strength, to pour through the straggling enemy forces that were being relentlessly battered from the ground and the air. The force of the drive carried the Combat Command through all resistance to Warmerville, east of Reims.

Simultaneous with CC"B"'s attacks to the east, CC"A" pressed on from Chateau-Thierry. They being the first Allied troops in this city, and having been the first of this conflict to see a battleground of the past war, perhaps a little inspiration was gained. The forces, so to speak, ran wild after crossing the Marne.

Lt. Col. McConnell's task force, still holding win money among CC"A"'s forces, led, spreading ruin and death in its wake. This force reached, fought for, and won Fismes. Two other forces from the Division raced to its support, and together they bore down on the Aisne River, north of the champagne capitol of Reims. Troops of CC"A" reached the banks of the river on the morning of August 29, and by nightfall had secured bridgeheads over it at Pontavert, Neufchatel, and Berry.

Not only had the first Allied bridgehead been secured across the Aisne, but numbers 2 and 3 as well.

Reims, prize city, and key to Germans trying to escape from the west, was encircled, and its loss to the enemy can be attributed to the 7th Armored Division.

This smashing attack had been a remarkable display of American armor. An enhancing factor was the rain, which had made the countryside a mass of absorbing gumbo. Regardless, Reims had been lost by the Germans.

A change of direction was ordered; there was at least one more river to cross. The 7th Armored Division was directed to press eastward to capture Verdun.

At Reims, a few C-47 transport planes had delivered a little fuel, but the tanks of the hundreds of vehicles of the 7th were far from full as columns sped toward Verdun. Col. Andrew J. Adams and his Division Trains personnel had expended superhuman efforts to keep the Division supplied. The 446th and 3967th Quartermaster Truck Companies raced continuously over recently conquered territory in vain attempts to keep vital stocks within reach of the combat elements, but supply lines were stretched almost to a breaking point, and distances were too great.

On the afternoon of August 29, the forces of CC"A" and CC"B" moved out from their assemblies near the little French town of Belne, east of Reims to attack Verdun, fortress city on the Meuse River, sacred to the hearts of many French patriots, and tactically important to the German Army.

CC"B"'s gasoline supply was exhausted before the troops reached the objective. The north flank drive had

12

lost its potency; vehicles of the command were halted in the center of the shell-marked trench-lined battle-fields of World War I near the Argonne Forest. However secondhand, the trenches served in good stead to protect the troops of the formation.

CC"A", on the south flank, had fuel left, little enough though it was. Some of the vehicles stopped, but enough carried on to reach Verdun. The for-tress city presented a formidable picture to the advancing forces, and the fire of German 88mm guns added immensely to the picture. The lead tank of Lt. Col. McConnell's force was knocked out at the city's edge, and enemy fire fell much too con-stantly. Artillery fire from Divisional units was brought to bear on the enemy's positions east of the town, and the troops were able to fight their way into heart of the city.

Shortly after noon on August 31, forces reached the main bridge over the Meuse in Verdun — and crossed it! Mines that had been emplaced in

Citizens of VERDUN, France, named a street for the 7th Armored Division.

13

the bridge structure had been deactivated by French patriots before the arrival of 7th Armored Division troops, and before a scared enemy garrison had been able to demolish the prize.

The City of Verdun, liberated by the 7th Armored, was taken without inflicting casualties upon the civil populus, and little material damage was necessary. The Division had accomplished its assigned mission; there was a secure bridgehead over the Meuse. (Appreciative citizens of Verdun later renamed the famous city street, • Rue de Chevert, for the Division — "Rue de la 7eme Division Blindeé, USA").

*

During the previously accounted three-week sweep, the 7th Armored Division rolled some 600 miles (65 miles was the record for one day), and during that 21-day period (August 10 to August 31), the 7th liberated approximately 150 French towns with an aggregate population of over 350,000. The toll on the enemy had been heavy, but the heaviest losses that the German had suffered were the river lines — barriers — that he had hoped to use to delay the advancing Allied Armies. The spearheading 7th Armored had wrecked his plans — from Normandy to Verdun — World War I famous city No. 2 to be taken by the Division's troops.

*

For six long days the 7th Armored waited at Verdun for gasoline; it waited because there was nothing else to do. While it waited, it held its ground, and planned, and sweated out the Nazi planes that came over at night to bomb the Verdun bridge, trying to wreck what the 7th had fought for and won.

14

Word came down from XX Corps that the Division would, when it got gasoline, advance to the east in multiple columns to seize crossings over the Moselle River at Metz, France. There were many things that didn't meet the eye on this planned junket, and there were enough things visible to discourage the doughtiest. The weather was bad; it had rained for days, and the terrain was highly unfavorable to armored operations.

What the troops couldn't see from their areas around Verdun were the minutely laid out perimeter defenses of the city of Metz. The Metz locale was honeycombed with concrete forts that were so old the earth had almost swallowed them into her makeup, but they had

Vehicles of the 87th Cav Rcn Squadron (Mecz) pass a demolished bridge near M E T Z, France, over a road being repaired by engineers.

been modernized by the enemy, and interconnecting underground passages were numerous. Moreover, the whole perimeter approach to Metz was dominated by the city's garrison; artillery pieces looked down from every fort and from every high, point of ground. The garrison consisted of the students and faculty of a military school located there, and every member had fought school problems over the whole area that had to be conquered. As has been said, there was a lot that didn't meet the eye.

Four columns of a reconnaissance force, under Lt. Col. Vincent L. Boylan, moved out from assembly areas in the early morning hours of September 6. The northernmost column reached the Moselle north of Metz, but was driven back by heavy artillery fire from German pieces sited on the opposite shores — on commanding ground. Other columns failed to reach the river line; they met steady fire from anti-tank guns and mortars, centered around the little villages of Gravelotte and St. Privat. The resistance was too heavy for the units committed, so the Combat Commands were assigned the mission of crossing the Moselle.

When the 7th hurled its strength against the renowned fortress city, it was the first American Division to batter at the place — the first of several to pour brave men into a bitter, lengthy battle.

For heartbreaking days and nights, in continued rainy weather that denied the Division much-needed air support, troops hammered at the monstrous bastion. Lack of heavy artillery support, and limited observation further restricted progress. The 7th's drive was admittedly slowed, but never stopped. With never-ending

16

effort and with constant display of individual bravery the troops moved ahead, almost inch by inch. The fort's guns poured murderous fire into occupied positions, and the students of the Metz Military School, fighting over the ground they knew so well with a fanaticism reportedly injected by Himmler himself, clung like leeches, and had to be bored out like them.

Finally, after overcoming all of the bitterest of opposition, the troops of the Division reached the Moselle south of Metz, and near the French hamlet of Dornot marked up another distinction for the command by forcing a crossing of the river and establishing a bridgehead and holding it against fanatic Germans and in the face of more artillery pounding directed on the bridge site from the nearby heights and from commanding forts. This crossing was made in conjunction with the 5th Infantry Division, but 7th Armored men were the first across the muddy Moselle on the Night of Sept. 8, 1944. There were more heroes in those days of action than one can count, but most important, the units were collectively heroic.

The heavy fighting and the inch-by-inch progress continued after the Moselle was bridged. The Division fought from hill mass to hill mass, from town to town, killing the enemy that barred the way and destroying his machines. Every inch of ground was contested; every inch was fought for and won. Prisoners were few; the battlefields were dotted with enemy dead.

Troops of the Division had fought their way to the Seille River, well to the east of the Moselle, when orders arrived on September 24, which carried it to Holland.

HOLLAND

The 7th moved rapidly across Belgium, and some troops saw Luxembourg as they marched on to Holland, to see that picture — book country, battered by the warring men that had traversed her soil.

The Division became a part of the First US Army, and was assigned the mission of clearing the Peel Swamp west of the Maas (Meuse) River. Vortum, Holland was attacked on September 30, with CC B as the striking force. Along the route to the town, the troops met strong anti-tank gun and enemy bazooka fire and overcame it, wiping out the defenders and rolling on. The leading elements captured Vortum on October 2, and the 7th had liberated its first Holland town.

Overloon, another small town, was attacked by CC A simultaneously with "B's" attack on Vortum. It was a much more difficult task — the taking of this Overloon town. It was heavily defended by Germans paratroops and former German Air Force personnel, fighting from well prepared positions. CC A's attack was made with two forces, one attacking from the northwest and the other from the southwest. One Task Force was commanded by Lt. Col. Richard D. Chappuis of the 48th Armored Infantry Battalion; the other fought under Major John C. Brown, 40th Tank Battalion.

The going was tough; there were no two ways about it. Tanks, canalized as they were on the roads through the swampy area, were held up by carefully sited anti-tank weapons. A lot of the enemy's guns were knocked out, but there seemed always to be others "just around the corner". The infantry, however, battled its way to the outskirts of Overloon during the late afternoon of

October 1. The doughboys were under heavy artillery fire, as they had been all the way to the town, and there were a lot of Nebelwerfers ("Screaming Meemies") to contend with, too, but they dug in to defend what they had fought so hard to gain.

On October 3, CC R moved up to attack Overloon from the North. One task force, commanded by Lt. Col. John P. Wemple, 17th Tank Battalion, ran into trouble — plenty of it. The troops hit a minefield that temporarily stymied them, and artillery and mortar fire poured in on them. Forward progress came to a halt. A second task force, commanded by Lt. Col. William H. Fuller, 38th Armored Infantry Battalion, moved nearer the town, and fought through a wooded area about a quarter of a mile north of Overloon. Enemy fire held the force there.

Linemen of the 147th Armd Sig Co repair lines "somewhere in Holland".

19

Further attacks on the town (one made at night) were halted by every conceivable means of defense known to the enemy. There were minefields, wire barricades, elaborate dugouts and entrenchments, and supporting them all was deadly cross fire from German machine guns and rifles. The mortar and artillery fire was incessant. The men of the 38th and 48th Armored Infantry Battalions, entrenched as they were, often were within grenade throwing distance of entrenched enemy troops. The enemy counter attacked constantly. Foxholes exchanged hands in hand-to-hand fighting — bayonets and grenades were the weapons of those days. The fires of the 434th, 440th and 489th Armored Field Artillery Battalions were unable to get at the enemy while he remained in his entrenchments and dugouts, but when the Germans rose to counterattack, the artillery fire, plus the fire of the troops on the ground, cut them down — killed them by the hundreds. On October 4, seven separate and distinct enemy counterattacks were thrown back at a terrific cost to the Germans, and without the 7th losing any of its previously gained positions. On October 8, the division was assigned to another Army — this time the British Second, under command of Lt. Gen. Miles C. Dempsey. General Dempsey had a more important mission for us, that of protecting the vital right flank of the British-Canadian drive to clear the northern and western approaches to the strategically important port of Antwerp. (The 7th armored is now officially credited with saving this campaign from possible disaster.)

The Division's mission was purely defensive — a new role for this armored force — and it was disposed accordingly. There were a few battles to gain ground more advantageous to the defense, and there were local victories gained by the 7th, but for the most part the command was spread out fanlike across the canal-stripped flatlands — watching, patrolling, keeping alert. On October 27, the 7th was spread thin over a 22 mile front, hinged in the center on Meijel, and stretching to both north and south on canal lines. The "line", so called, consisted of a number of outposts of a few men each, sometimes as much as 800 yards apart. German patrols had been active, and the weather had kept Allied air patrols on the ground. Enemy Intelligence evidently had become well informed as to the Division's precarious position, for it was at this time that the

Medical personnel of the 77th Armd Med Bn administer the wounds of a stricken comrade, and inject life-giving plasma into his blood stream.

German launched his now famous counterattack designed to disrupt British operations on Antwerp. The German did not, however, with all his carefully laid plans, give full enough consideration to the fighting spirit of the separated groups of the American 7th Armored, or their collective potency.

As soon as the strength of the counterattack became known, Gen. Dempsey ordered additional forces into the battle, and asked the 7th to hold until they arrived. The battle raged bitterly for three days; the 7th Armored, outnumbered three-to-one, conceded little ground — and killed a lot of Germans.

The counterattack started with a thundering hour and ten minute artillery barrage directed at the 87th Cavalry Reconnaissance Squadron, Mechanized, which was holding the center of the Division's zone. Three simultaneous infantry attacks followed, with the enemy pouring across the separating canal under heavy artillery support. The heaviest blow was directed at Meijel, where there were only two platoons to meet the enemy forces approaching under a heavy fog which cut down fields of fire to as low as 40 yards.

Flank platoons were ordered into the fight, but seriously outnumbered and hampered by zero visibility, the 7th's men were forced slowly back. Other enemy attacks, to the north and south of Meijel, had been contained by groups of men who refused to give ground in the face of odds. Lt. Col. Boylan's 87th Cavalry Squadron launched two counterattacks against Meijel during the morning, but the enemy had used his time well and had a strong enough force in the town to hold off the attackers.

CC R, commanded by Col. John L. Ryan, Jr., was ordered to take over the Meijel sector. An afternoon attack by the 48th Armored Infantry Battalion was thwarted by an enemy attack in the opposite direction. Many of the troops were cut off by German tanks, which had been put across the canal to support the enemy infantry. The threat of encirclement forced a withdrawal to more advantageous positions. Meanwhile, the enemy hordes were streaming across the canal; an attack near Heitrak, north of Meijel, which was supported by 20 enemy tanks, was stopped cold by D troop, 87th Cavalry Reconnaissance Squadron and two companies of armor from the 17th Tank Battalion.

With the line of the Division shortened, CC B attacked along the Liesel-Meijel road on October 28. After an advance of 3500 yards, resistance stiffened to a dregee that compelled the 23d Armored Infantry Battalion to dig in and hold on grimly to protect its gain. A planned secondary thrust, down the Asten-Meijel road.

Maintenance men of the 129th Ord Bn replace an engine in a battleworn tank of the Division.

23

was cancelled because of the heavy pressure that was being exerted to the front and infiltrations into positions of the 48th Armored Infantry Battalion that threatened the security of the left flank of CC R. Defense was maintained during the remainder of the day and night.

The Germans struck again on October 29, pushing an armored column with heavy infantry support into Liesel, cutting the main line of communication with the 23rd Armored Infantry Battalion. Enemy artillery support for all of the operations in this counterattack was heavy and the armor was bountiful. Prisoners yielded the information that the forces involved were the crack 9 Panzer Division and the 15 Panzer Grenadier Division, plus thousands of oddments — mostly engineers and former Luftwaffe personnel.

As the one enemy column struck through to reach Liesel, another attacked to the north — toward Asten — and with a vastly superior force of tanks and infantry, was able to make a slight penetration of the lines of the 48th. Determined troops in newly established strongpoints to the rear of the initial line of contact broke up this attack, and stopped the thrust. The approaches to Asten were denied the Germans.

The defensive positions established by the 7th were consolidated, and were taken over after dusk on the 29th by the reinforcing troops Gen. Dempsey had promised. The gallant men of the Division had accomplished the assigned mission. At no time during those three days was a superior German force able to crack the will or the lines of the Units of CC B and CC R. There had been withdrawals, granted, but that was with a view to economy of personnel, and the mission in mind. The big thing was that the Germans had not got through!

Much of the credit for halting the Germans was due Col. Orville W. Martin's Division Artillery, which was augmented by British units. Each thrust made by the enemy had been met with massed, destructive fire; the dead Germans that littered the battlefield were proof of its effectiveness. When the enemy infiltrated artillery positions, cannoneers took up rifles to beat the Germans off — yes, the artillery did a mighty fine job. One Jerry infantry battalion, preparing to move out against CC R from a wooded area north of Meijel was rendered completely ineffective by artillery fire; prisoners from that group backed up that fact. And on the night

M7 of 7th Armored Division Field Artillery fires a battalion's 100,000th round in operations on the Continent.

of October 28, a box barrage that was laid down allowed two companies of the 48th Armored Infantry Battalion to get out of a position that had been completely cut off from friendly troops.

When the 7th was relieved, the British VIII Corps, under which it had been fighting, ordered it to take over a very much narrowed sector south of Meijel, centering on the little canal junction town of Nederweert,

Brig. Gen. R. W. Hasbrouck former CG of Combat Command B, assumed command of the 7th Armored Division on November 1. (He was promoted to the rank of Major General on February 9, 1945.)

In expression of appreciation for the stand that the division made at Meijel, Gen. Dempsey, Commander of the British Second Army, wrote the following in a letter to Gen. Hasbrouck:

"I congratulate you all on the splendid way in which you held off the strong enemy attack which came against you at Meijel. You were heavily outnumbered, but, by holding firm, as you did, you gave me ample time to bring up the necessary reserves. I appreciate the high fighting qualities which your division showed."

The enemy was dug in every where, and in addition, they had strewn mines of every description promiscuously over the landscape, making our initial advances slow. From across the canal Du Nord, 7th's southern boundary, came fire from dug-in tanks and artillery. The British air support and the 7th's artillery soon silenced these harassing forces and the attacks speeded on towards Meijel. Soggy Holland fields and pure swampland prohibited wide use of armor. The 7th fought an infantry battle. Within sight of Meijel on 6 November, the 7th Armored Division was ordered to the 9th US Army.

Thus ended the 7th's Holland campaign.

26

GERMANY AND THEN ST. VITH

While the Division as an entity remained in rest during the remainder of November — the first relief from combat since August 14, the Division Artillery moved up to support offensive operations of the units in the XIII Corps zone. Other units, too, fought with neighboring divisions. The 40th Tank Battalion worked with the 84th Infantry Division and on November 29 captured Lindern, Germany and repulsed several German counterattacks before the arrival of the supporting infantry. On December 1, elements of Col. Wemple's 17th Tank Battalion moved in with troops of the 102nd Infantry

Cub plane of the 7th Armored Division Artillery takes off on a runway that was cleared among snowdrifts.

Division to take Linnich, Germany, located on the banks of the now famous Roer River.

The entire. Division moved into Germany, and there followed a period of intensive planning in preparation for participation in the Ninth US Army's drive into the Rhineland, over the Roer River and deeper into the heart of the Reich. It was during this period that the maintenance crews of the 129th Ordnance Battalion, commanded by Lt. Col. George Hughes, were able, for the first time since the beginning of the campaign, to spend much-needed time in making necessary repairs to combat vehicles of the Division — to make every vehicle of the command ready for the next mission. All this while, the troops of the Division were experiencing conditions inside the enemy's homeland — a battered generality, a subdued and curiously dangerous looking civil population, and eternal mud.
It was while the Division was thusly making itself ready for offensive action that it got alert orders — orders to move quickly and without warning of what was to follow to the general area of Vielsalm-St. Vith, Belgium, far to the South.

General Hasbrouck was at his headquarters at Castle Rimburg, just inside the German border near battered Ubach, when he got the movement orders late on Saturday afternoon, December 16.

The first troops were on the road in a very few hours, heading towards the American VIII Corps sector on what everyone believed was to be a routine road march to a new assembly area. Within 12 hours after the first troops started their movement, and after a move of over 50 miles, they were battling a ferocious enemy

28

in territory reported to have been held by friendly troops.

That was the prosaic start of what became an epic stand in American military history — the stand of the 7th Armored Division at ST. VITH, Belgium, in the face of Field Marshal Von Rundstedt's now famous "winter offensive."

When the troops of the 7th Armored went into position around ST. VITH. a vital road and rail center, it was evident that the town would fall to the Germans unless the Division could do something about it. And do something, it did; it held through five bloody, embattled days, while Allied forces were marshalled from far and near to hold the enemy's big counter-offensive.

Officers and men of the 23rd Armd Inf Bn move up between deep snowbanks south of BORN, Belgium.

The enemy forces, carefully hoarded and gathered by the German High Command, and commanded by the battle-wise von Rundstedt, had run rampant over American positions since early morning December 16. The Wehrmacht and SS troops had been told that they were going to retake the port of Antwerp, and that they would spend New Year's eve in Paris. The first objective was Liege, and the path to it ran through ST. VITH — and the 7th Armored.

The Division was now with the First US Army, and had made its very rapid appearance on its fourth battle front — all widely separated. Little wonder that the confused enemy staffs called it "The Ghost Division." (American correspondents referred to it as the "Rattlesnake" Division; *"you could never tell where it was going to strike next".)*

The 7th's line was built up methodically as the troops arrived in the area — some of them having had to fight their way in the Division's sector. Although established piecemeal as units arrived, the defensive position was extremely well organized and held the Germans off. The line was somewhat akin to a horseshoe, extending from north and west of ST VITH to east of that town, and then to the south of it and westward. The troops of th 7th held the north and east portions; into the defenses built along the south rim were CC B of the 9th Armored Division, the 424th Regiment of the seriously decimated 106th Infantry Division, and the 112th Regimental Combat Team of the 28th Infantry Division, which had been splintered from its parent division by a thrust by German forces south of St. Vith. All these forces eventually fought under General Hasbrouck's command, as did the 14th Cavalry Group, the

30

275th Armored Field Artillery Battalion and other units that had lost their parent organizations in the initial phases of the German drive.

The enemy hit the positions of the 7th and were fought off, only to strike again. When the German found he couldn't make any headway against the Division's troops, he began to peel off to the north and the south, probing continually in an attempt to get inside the "horseshoe". He didn't get in, but the men and machines felt the weight of his thrusts; there were plenty of times when everybody wondered when something would have to give.

That the 7th's stand was recognized even in its earlier phases became known when Gen. Hasbrouck received this message from General Dwight D. Eisenhower, Supreme Commander of Allied Troops in the ETO!

"The magnificient job that you are doing is having a great beneficial effect on our whole situation. I am personally grateful to you and wish you would let all of your people know that if they continue to carry out their mission with the splendid spirit they have so far shown, they will have deserved well of their country."

(Five panzer divisions, three Volks-grenadier divisions, and the Gross Deutschland Brigade were identified in contact with the Division during the course of the St. Vith struggle. Minimum estimates placed the enemy strength employed against the 7th at various times as over 100,000 men and at least 500 armored vehicles, most of which were tanks.)

There was no time to ponder over how grateful was their country by the troops in the line. Basically, they held a line, and their orders were to continue holding it, and out front there was an enemy — a very numerous, aggressive, and fanatic enemy. The dead piled up in front of the 7th's positions, and enemy vehicles were being knocked out all over the place, but the German kept coming. He was very determined to get through — ahead lay Liege — and Paris! The horseshoe held its form.

The enemy employed a "bouncing ball" technique to probe for a weak spot in the line of the 7th Armored and its attached units. With each "bounce", limited reserves were shifted from within the confines of the horseshoe line to strike back at that point of the perimeter where the enemy hit. The enemy troops, failing to penetrate the line, would slide by the 7th, to both the north and south. On the south, there was nothing between the Division and the 101st Airborne Division at Bastogne. The Germans slid on by and drove to the west. On the north, some enemy passed by the Division's perimeter and also moved to the west. The overall position of the 7th began to look like a strange peninsula of will power and guts jutting out into a sea of hate and fanaticism. To say that is was a precarious position is putting it lightly.

The western drive along the southern perimeter brought enemy forces in contact with 7th "rear" installations. In those embittered days, there existed no line of demarkation between rear and front. Division trains personnel, organized by Col. Adams, stepped out of character — became fighting troops, and established defensive positions and road blocks. And they killed a lot of Germans, and held more off. The heaviest action by the Trains centered around Samree and La Roche, and as certainly as the action at the so called "front" fitted into the organization that blunted von Rundstedt's drive.

The troops along the eastern end of the horseshoe had been forced to ration their almost exhausted stocks of gasoline, food, and ammunition. The arrival of an armored supply column that had zigzagged through the maze of enemy infiltrations from Marche to Salmchateau alleviated that worry for the time being, and gave the desperately fighting troops temporary hope.

The expected blow fell on December 21. German commanders had been building up their forces for four days, and circumstance prohibited any effective countermeasures. Zero visibility prohibited air support; troops could not be spared from one portion of the line to strengthen another. When the enemy forces struck at CC B's lines east of ST. VITH on that day, hostile strength was too great; the Germans withstood the heavy losses suffered and still kept coming. The gallant troops gave way, reluctantly, and were shifted to a new, precariously thin line west of the town. Again forced to fall back, Brig. Gen. Clarke brilliantly and magically established a new line east of Kromback by a magnificient display of courage and leadership.

Another ferocious and powerful drive was launched by the enemy on December 22 — from the east and from the north, at the junction of the sectors held by CC B and CC A. The latter had been continually engaged with extremely aggressive forces in a see-saw battle for Poteau. Pressure on the entire salient increased, and as practically no lines of communication existed, higher headquarters ordered the 7th to withdraw. Bitter cold, in which the troops had been fighting, had added to all other difficulties. For once — for the withdrawal, it was a benefit. Frozen earth permitted heavy vehicles to traverse otherwise impossible routes.

The withdrawal began during the early morning hours of December 23. Had the "book" been consulted, it would have been found that daylight withdrawals are treated only in the "impossible" chapter. Of that it can be said, therefore, that the 7th Armored accomplished the impossible!

Units disengaged one by one; meticulously laid plans were executed. The troops moved cautiously over three narrow routes to the Salm River to the only two available crossings. One crossing, however, was denied the Division later in the day by German columns that cut the escape route west of the river. Covering forces to the east, west, and south fought bitter rearguard actions as the enemy pressed hard on the retiring Division's heels. There were many units represented in these forces, and all their gallant work was magnificient, but the work of elements of the 814th Tank Destroyer Battalion, attached to the 7th in Normandy and now considered an integral part of the command, was particularly outstanding. The guns of the battalion slugged it out with the fast-clinging panzers, and kept them off the columns as they moved carefully and surely, across the Salm.

For this withdrawal, an elaborate artillery schedule was planned, and the fires of every available piece kept the enemy hordes at bay while the troops left the area — to move across the river into comparative safety of the sector to the west.

It would be extremely false to say that the 7th was

34

VITAL STATISTICS
(The following figures apply up to and including VE Day only.)

The 7th Armored Division
(The Division travelled 2,260 combat miles.)

Supply

Gasoline consumed —
3, 127, 151 gallons

Ammunition expended —

105mm	350,027	rounds
76mm	19,209	,,
75mm	48,724	,,
.50 Cal	1,267,128	,,
.45 Cal	540,523	,,
.30 Cal	9,367,966	,,

Decorations

Distinguished Service Crosses	10
Silver Stars	351
Bronze Star Medals	
(1) Heroic Action	898
(2) Meritorious Service	1,047
Purple Hearts	1,211

(The above listed number of Purple Hearts is exclusive of those awarded by the War Department and non-divisional medical installations.)

Battle Participation

Campaign of Northern France
11. August 1944 to 14 September 1944)

Rhineland Campaign
(15. December 1944 to 21 March 1945)

Ardennes Campaign
(16 December 1944 to 25 January 1945)

Campaign of Central Germany
(22 March 1945 to VE Day)

The Opposing German Forces

During the course of battle, the 7th Armored exacted this toll against the opposing enemy formations — —

113,041 prisoners captured
   621 Armored vehicles destroyed.
    89 Armored vehicles captured.
2,653 Miscellaneous Vehicles destroyed.
3,517 Miscellaneous Vehicles captured.
   583 pieces of armament (larger than 50mm) destroyed.
   361 pieces of armament (larger than 50mm) captured.

THE 7th ARMORED WHIPPED THE GERMANS WHIPPED THEM BY . . .

SMASHING OPPOSITION

A tank of the Division rolls by the flaming wreckage of a German vehicle it has just hit in an advance on the Ruhr Pocket.

DESTROYING EQUIPMENT

Tail end of a column that forces of the Division overtook and knocked out near KUNKLOP, Germany.

KILLING AND CAP-TURING THE ENEMY

One of several columns of prisoners streaming back along roads behind the 7th Armored in the vicinity of LANGEN-HOLTEN, Germany.

WHERE THERE WAS TROUBLE, THE 7th ARMORED WENT . . .

In France there was CHARTRES, MELUN, EPERNAY, and METZ. And then to Holland -- OVERLOON, LIESEL, MIEJEL.

TO BELGIUM
(St Vith - Manhay)

From a dug-in position north of MANHAY, Belgium, a tank destroyer of the 814th T. D. Bn keeps watch over the village which saw heavy, bitter fighting on Christmas Day, 1944.

And to GERMANY
(Giessen, Kirchain, Eder See Dam, Ruhr Pocket)

Troops of the Division raise OLD GLORY over the EDER SEE Dam, which was captured intact by the 7th.

It travelled so fast and so mysteriously that the Germans called it "The Ghost"; correspondents called it the "Rattlesnake Division" not hurt in this battle of ST. VITH. It was hurt badly, as a mortal can be hurt — the men were dogtired and fewer than they were on December 17th, and many of the vehicles and the weapons that had gone into the battle had been lost. The Division needed the chance to rest, to get back into shape again, to lick its wo unds, and that chance was expected as it pulled back into assembly areas. The dictates of war are cruel and relentless — the division was committed to action again in the early evening hours of December 24th — on Christmas Eve night!

The enemy had lunged anew, and once more the 7th was thrown in the German's path, to plug a gap at the little crossroads town of Manhay, on Highway 15, whose

Mortar crew of the 38th Armd Inf Bn in action north of ST VITH, Belgium.

35

paved lanes ran straight to Liege — again the enemy's objective.

An enemy force, strong with armor (some of it captured American equipment), pushed 2,000 yards north of Manhay in the early hours before Christmas dawn. CC A, with 424th Infantry Regiment attached, engaged this force, and by midnight, after a Christmas Day full of fierce fighting, had pushed to the outskirts of Manhay, had occupied the high ground, 1,000 yards to the north of the town and had organized those heights for defense. American artillery rocked the town all day December 26, and early on the morning of December 27th, paratroopers and engineers attached to the 7th for the purpose, attacked Manhay. The town, battered by artillery that had cascaded on it for preceding hours, was taken by a bunch of determined men who routed the tenacious enemy out of the rubble — killing them or marching them to the prisoner of war cages. Tanks moved in to support the defensive positions established; the enemy had lost Manhay as he had lost the impetus of his entire winter offensive. To further support the defense, the guns of the Division's Artillery Command poured a never-ending stream of projectiles into the woods and on the roads south of the captured town. The Germans never came back!

*

On January 23, 1945, one month to the day after a division of weary warriors had been ordered to withdraw from St. Vith, the 7th Armored fought its way back into the now bomb-wrecked village.

The 7th's return to St. Vith climaxed a four-day drive from the north during which heavy opposition was beat

36

down in the bitterest kind of weather. Snow was everywhere, having drifted in some places to a depth of six feet. Through it, and through the positions of a determined enemy, the men and tanks of the 7th Armored pushed to St. Vith.

CC A, under Col. William S. Triplet, and CC B, commanded by General Bruce C. Clarke, began the attack on January 20th. On that first day, CC"A" captured DIEDENBERG, along with the few Germans that weren't left in the snow. CC"B" moved into position north and west of BORN to assault that town. BORN was well defended with plenty of German grenadiers and armor. It wasn't easy at all, the taking of that town. The troops worked their way up to the scarred village through a

Tanks of the 31st Tk Bn in position during the drive that took the Division back into ST VITH, Belgium.

hail of fire, moving through the deep snow, and entered it on January 21st. That entry didn't mean by a long shot that the Germans were through. They had to be dug out of the nooks and crannies in the roughest sort of house-to-house fighting. It was done, though, and the town was cleared by the end of the day; with its fall, a lot of prisoners were accounted for, as were several pieces of armor that had been dealing much too much misery.

Then, on January 22nd, troops scrambled on through the snow drifts, still under mortar and artillery fire, to seize the high ground to the north of ST. VITH. The enemy clung to this key point, and had to be routed — almost one by one. HUNNINGEN, a small village to the northwest of ST. VITH, also a scene of heavy fighting in the earlier battle, fell to the 7th Armored on January 22nd after a quick thrust by a bunch of daring tankers and doughboys that virtually wiped out the defending garrison. All this paved the way to ST. VITH. The only things between the 7th Armored and ST. VITH were snow, a lot of open ground that was covered by withering fire and a pot full of Germans that were holed up in the rubble of the town.

Columns started moving on ST. VITH early in the afternoon of January 23rd, after artillery had done some softening up of its defenders. Three forces moved on the town. The 23rd Armored Infantry Battalion moved across the open ground to the north of ST. VITH, with its left flank to the enemy, and was the first to enter the town. It entered the northeast corner of the town and established defensive positions there and northward to protect against enemy efforts.

38

A task force under Major William F. Beatty, 31st Tank Battalion, moved along the axis Hunningen — St. Vith, pushing along the main road. Another force, under Lt. Col. Chappuis, 48th Armored Infantry Battalion, pressed out to flank the town from the west, south of Major Beatty's force. These two forces, after battering their respective ways through stubborn enemy troops outposting the rubble that was St. Vith joined inside the town and methodically cleaned out the clinging Germans, withstanding, meanwhile, the weight of German artillery and mortar fire played on them from the high ground to the east.

Three and one-half hours after the attack jumped off, St. Vith was once again in 7th Armored Division hands! The Germans were reluctant to give up their erstwhile

33rd Armd Engr Bn men advertise the 7th Armored's return to ST VITH, Belgium on Jan. 23, '45.

valuable hub; four counterattacks were launched during the night that followed. The strongest was directed at the exposed flank of the 23rd Armored Infantry Battalion north of St. Vith, and was broken up by the accurate fire of Division and attached Artillery. The others were on a less intense scale, and were repulsed by the troops that had retaken the Belgian village with heavy losses suffered by the abortively directed enemy. The tenacity of the Germans came to greater light on January 24, when in final mopping up operations, a fairly high number of prisoners was taken from the battered buildings, after sniping through the darkness of the preceding night, some having infiltrated into their positions during the hours of darkness.

The 7th's capture of St. Vith marked the virtual demise of Von Rundstedt's winter offensive. The enemy forces had been battered back for 50 of the 55 miles that they had gained, and there losses of men and material had been high. The fields over which the soldiers of the Division fought bore mute testimony to the German losses. Vehicles and equipment of all descriptions that had been knocked out one month earlier strewed the ground, only to be added to by the new toll exacted by the weapons of the 7th in the recapture of the scene of its gallant, historic December stand.

When the Division had finished its job in the St. Vith area, it was pulled out of action and assembled in the Eupen, Belgium, area, where the men of the command were given the opportunity of resting and getting equipment back into combat shape. During the time that the Division as a whole was in the Eupen area, the 23rd Armored Infantry Battalion was attached to the 78th Infantry Division for a short period, as was CC"R",

40

under Col. Francis P. Tompkins. The troops of CC"R" aided the 78th in seizing the approaches to the very important Schwammenauel Dam, at the headwaters of the Roer River. The Division's artillery — 434th, 440th, and 489th Armored Field Artillery Battalions — also lent supporting fire to the infantry divisions engaged in combat missions in the area of the dam.

The men and guns of the 203rd AAA Bn protected the 7th Armd from air attacks during the entire campaign.

FROM THE ROER TO THE RHINE

On March 5, the 7th Armored moved up to aid in clearing the enemy from the territory west of the Rhine River. Collapse of general enemy resistance between the Roer and the Rhine left the 7th without a seriously defended objective, however, and simplified the job to a major degree. The only fighting that was of any consequence entered into by troops of the Division was in the area to the southwest of Bonn, where a stubborn pocket held out in an attempt to keep an escape avenue to the Rhine open. The pressure of the 7th's troops forced a collapse of this resistance; the offensive power of the Division could not be stemmed — the enemy it faced was destroyed.

While awaiting further assignment, the Division occupied the area around Bad Godesburg, a resort and health center on the West Bank of the Rhine, establishing control over the population and combing the area occupied for enemy soldiers who had been unable to escape across the Rhine. Nearly a thousand prisoners were taken during this period —- most of them having masqueraded in civilian clothes to escape their ultimate destiny. It was while the 7th Armored was deployed along the west bank of the Rhine that the 203rd AAA Battalion was called on to augment the anti-aircraft defense of the famous Remagen bridge. The 203rd, which had been attached to the 7th in Normandy, had seen all of the hardships that the Division had seen, and was to see all of those in the future; it was, for all practical purposes, one of the Division's own units. It added the weight of its weapons to the array that saved the Remagen bridge from the constant, but vain, attempts of the Luftwaffe.

42

OVER THE RHINE — INTO THE HEART
OF THE REICH

The 7th Armored went back into action on March 26 — into the sort of action for which it was designed — and with a vengeance.

Launching out as the center spearhead of a coordinated attack along the entire First Army front, the 7th broke out of the Remagen bridgehead, and drove on unchecked for five eventful days — roared on until it was ordered to halt. During those five days it led the offensive, bore the brunt of the resistance that the enemy offered, changed directions three times and covered 148 miles of German countryside, leaving it littered with the remains of a once-proud enemy fighting machine.

The drive was not unopposed; it was simply an impos-

Infantrymen of the Division quite often went into battle mounted on tanks, particularly in the dash from the Remagen bridgehead.

43

sibility for the Germans to successfully cope with the speed and daring of the Division's attack. There were stubborn defenses met at many points, and these defenses were completely crushed by the 7th's driving power.

On the initial day, Nazis manning the defensive positions along the Reichs Autobahn leading south to Limburg temporaily held up CC"R"; artillery blasted out the defenders of the approaches to the super-highway and allowed CC R" and CC"A" access to the road and its adjacent subsidiaries. After traveling at breakneck speed toward Limburg for a time, hammering aside all resistance that the Germans could muster, CC"A"'s columns veered to the east, as did CC"R"s forces to the north.

The second day also showed remarkable progress. Troops reached and crossed the Dill River, securing bridgeheads from which the next day they struck again due east. In reaching the Dill, columns had poured through huge sections of countryside infested with a feverishly frantic enemy. Task Force Brown, commanded by Lt. Col. John Brown of the 40th Tank Battalion, for example, had waded through heavily defended towns initially, battering down their defenses, and then had shaken completely loose and rampaged toward the Dill, churning through the retreating masses of two German divisions, leaving behind, as it roared onward, a mangled residue — the remains of the retreating enemy formations. Hundreds of vehicles were caught from behind, smashed, and left littering the roadside. Thousands of Germans laid down their arms in the face of this and the other columns. On the third day of the drive, troops of CC"A" captured Giessen, key railroad center far to the east of the Dill, neutralizing the fires of hundreds of anti-aircraft weapons that had been hastily transformed to a ground role, after having attempted to protect the city and its rail facilities against Allied air attacks for the past months. It was a bitter struggle, however brief, and represented an ultimate in daring and aggression; the vast quantity of anti-aircraft weapons was amazing — and they all lay smashed after the 7th rolled on.

Troops that pushed on slightly to the east of Giessen ran afoul of hordes of Germans retreating along the axis of the Autobahn to Kassel. 7th Armored Division troops were not ordered to reach and cut that arterial highway, but they struck near it, and the toll of prisoners and dead was enormous. The bewildered enemy showed little heart ro fight, and the smashing power of the 7th accentuated their distaste for further useless struggle.

A portion of the 1200 American soldiers liberated from the Germans east of W E T Z L A R, Germany, by the 7th Armored.

Swinging north on the fourth day of the drive, a new enemy was encountered, a Division just arrived from Denmark. Its troops were fresh, and their defensive positions good — but not good enough. This new German formation was defending a generally east-west line through Kirchain, with a great deal of its power in that town. They offered bitter opposition, and fought doggedly from position to position. They were beaten though — thoroughly beaten by the tanks and men of CC"R" with some assistance from CC"B". Kirchain was captured; the German 166th Infantry Division was, for all practical purposes, kaput!

The climax to the drive from the Rhine came on the fifth day. The Division bowled over all resistance to reach — and capture intact — the great Eder See Dam, 25 miles north of Kirchain. By nightfall, troops of CC B, now commanded by Col. John E. Haskell, and CC R, were occupying the south bank of the enormous lake. Outpost positions were established north of the dam itself — across the lake. The Eder See Dam — holding back the largest water capacity in all Europe — was uncontestably a 7th Armored Division prize. The enormous structure, measuring 400 meters in length and 48 meters in height, with its 15 generator turbines, would no longer supply the war production plants through the industrial section from Frankfurt to Hanover, nor could its gates be opened to flood the valley of the Eder River and hold up the American advance.

This five-day dash represented the ultimate in an armored division's effectiveness. All points of resistance had been neutralized; the enemy's will to fight was broken, and his material power smashed. Thousands of prisoners were herded to the rear; other thousands surrendered to infantry divisions which followed up the 7th as it tore through the enemy's ranks.

This drive provided one of the most difficult of all the problems that had been faced by the Division's signal component. The columns raced faster than the men of the 147th Armored Signal Company, commanded by Capt. Joseph Benson, could establish adequate signal communications facilities. Those men, however, who had more often than not braved enemy fire to install lines and stations to get "the message through", improvised and raced with the columns, established relays and kept messengers roaring over the littered

Men of the 48th Armd Inf Bn fan out to survey the countryside when the road near D E E K E N B A C K, Germany, is blocked by K O'd enemy vehicles.

47

roads; it was rare indeed when the signals didn't get through.

Prior to crossing the Rhine, the 7th Armored had captured 9,045 prisoners; the Germans taken by the Division during the five-day rampage numbered 13,071. Leading elements could do little more than disarm them and start them marching rearward, to be picked up and impounded by following formations. In addition to Germans captured, there was an untold number of foreign nationals liberated, both prisoners of war and "slave" laborers. Former prisoners of the Nazis, soldiers of France, Belgium, Russia, Holland, Yugoslavia, Poland, and Czechoslavakia lined the country roads and the village streets and waved the 7th Armored onward. Two prison camps and one marching column of American and British were overrun. Thousands of Yanks and Tommies were freed, including seven former members of the 7th Armored.

The pause in the Eder See area was brief; the pocket around the Ruhr industrial area had been closed and orders came for the 7th to aid in wiping out an estimated 100,000 Wehrmacht cornered there. CC A was the first element of the Division to go into action against the pocket, under attachment to the 9th Infantry Division. For an outstanding job with this neighboring division, CC A received the warmest praise from the Commanding General of the 9th.

On April 5, the 7th went into action, attacking, from a southwesterly direction, the pocket it had helped to create. The enemy was fighting in a sector well adapted to the defense, and he was desperate in his defense of every point of terrain, watching keenly, and massing

48

troops for, a chance to break out. As was said at the time, the forces were fighting on a "one-tank front", battering slowly through narrow defiles, destroying the defenses that had been set up astride the mountain roads.

The Germans defended everything — roads, ridges, towns, stream lines, and fought to gain back anything they lost. Despite their cunning and elaborate use of the many natural defensive positions, the 7th Armored pushed relentlessly onward. The troops took Schmallenberg, Gleidorf, Fredeburg — and two score other villages that are hard to find on a map. They took them, because they were all occupied and defended; they held them

Tanks of the 40th Tk Bn move into position in the debris of the newly-taken town of N E I D E R S-O R P E, Germany.

when the enemy counterattacked. Centered as it was on the Ruhr industrial section, shortened lines of communication gave the enemy the advantage of supply; there always seemed to be ample ammunition. Projectiles rained unceasingly on 7th Armored Division positions. The anti-aircraft weapons that had been emplaced for protection of the Ruhr against Allied air attack were converted to ground use, and were in evidence everywhere.

In this battle, as there are, unfortunately, in all phases of combat, there were casualties, and the cry of a wounded man for "Medic" never went unheeded. The aid men of the assault echelons, and the battalion aid stations, and all medical installations, for that matter, pressed unceasingly their humanitarian labors, under terrifically adverse and hazardous conditions. The 77th Medical Battalion, with its collecting and clearing agencies, and with its hospital facilities, cared for the wounded, and saw to it that every possible aid was given every man who had suffered bodily harm at the hand of the German. The haven of the Geneva Red Cross will not soon be forgot by those unfortunate members of the 7th Armored whose blood was spilled on the fields of battle.

The 7th pushed on. The prisoner take grew larger, and the German's attitude lapsed to that of defense only; little aggressive action was encountered, but there was never a decrease in the intensity of the fighting. There always seemed to be ample manpower, ample armor, ample everything. It was readily apparent that original estimates of 100,000 troops in the pocket was low; the 7th alone took over 45,000 prisoners while engaged in this operation.

50

The staff of the German LXXXI Corps was captured on April 12 by the 17th Tank Battalion. The 87th Cavalry Reconnaissance Squadorn (Mecz) captured the Corps Commander, a lieutenant General, on the following morning. These Germans expressed admiration and fear of the 7th Armored's aggressiveness and power, and for themselves had little to say except "Alles Kaput".

In order to gain deception and to utilize more suitable terrain the Division changed direction to the north as the attack progressed. On April 14, CC Λ fought its way into Hemer, and freed 23,000 former Allied soldiers, mostly Russian, from one of the largest prison camps to be overrun in the war by any force. The deplorable conditions that existed in that camp brought harshly to mind the brutality of the enemy that the 7th was fighting.

The eastern part of the pocket collapsed when early on the morning of the 16th, a German representative came into lines of the 38th Armored Infantry Battalion,

A 7th Armored infantryman covers Germans who came across the fields near R O D- H E I M , Germany, to surrender to him.

51

west of Menden, stating that he wished to discuss terms of surrender. In order to save time in effecting the surrender, Col. John L. Ryan, Jr., 7th Armored Division Chief of Staff, went to an enemy Corps Command Post behind the enemy lines as a representative of General Hasbrouck. There Col. Ryan told the commander of the Corps (LIII) that the 7th was poised for the attack, ·delivered the unconditional surrender terms, and gave the Nazi Commanders 15 minutes to arrive at a decision. Within seven minutes the terms were accepted, bringing a complete collapse to the eastern half of the Ruhr pocket.

As a result of this negotiation, which entailed the surrender of the LIII Corps — including the 116 Panzer Division, 180 Infantry Division, 190 Infantry Division, the remnants of the 9th Panzer Division and the Corps staff, 20,302 prisoners were taken into custody

A few of the thousands of prisoners captured by the 7th Armored in the Ruhr pocket.

by the 7th Armored Division on that eventful day of
April 16.

*

*An Army's death is a pitiful sight, but there were no
tears shed by the men of the 7th Armored when the
once-mighty Wehrmacht collapsed. To bring that collapse
to realization, the Division had long played a vital,
dramatic, and bloody part, and it was ready to do more
when resistance vanished.*

HEADQUARTERS III CORPS
Office of the Commanding General
APO 303, U. S Army

6 May 1945

Major General Robert W. Hasbrouck,
Commanding General, 7th Armored Division
APO 257, U. S. Army

My dear General Hasbrouck:

I want to thank you and the officers and men of your splendid
division for their magnificent and outstanding work while operating
under the III Corps. The III Corps was pleased to have you assigned
on 7 March 1945 and regretted exceedingly when you passed to other
control on 17 April. The great successes of the 7th Armored
Division during this period will, I am sure, stand out as brilliant
pages in the military operations on the Western Front.

From 7 March to 24 March the 7th Armored Division defended from
the west bank the bridgehead over the Rhine River at Remagen. On
24 March it moved east of the Rhine, and on the morning of 26 March
broke out of the bridgehead and attacked east in one of the most
rapid and vicious advances by armor which has ever been executed by
American forces. In three days and nights your division advanced
relentlessly 70 miles to seize the important center of Giessen and
the road centers northeast thereof. In this advance the division
overcame innumerable obstacles, strong enemy action of all types,
effected without delay a change of objectives from the city of Limburg
to Giessen and captured intact vital river crossings, great quantities
of enemy materiel and supplies, thousands of prisoners of war and re-
covered thousands of Allied prisoners of war. This advance spear-
headed the drive of the First Army, and furnishes a classic example
of the correct use of armor.

On 29 March the division was directed to change its attack from
east to north. Attacking boldly, the division again covered great
distances, overcame severe resistance, seized the dam at Ederstau
See and assisted in completing the encirclement of the Ruhr Basin.

On 3 April the III Corps was given the mission of attacking into
the Ruhr pocket from the east and the 7th Armored Division was assigned
the center zone. Despite bitter enemy resistance and almost impassable
mountainous terrain, the 7th Armored Division attacked with infantry

54

and armor at strong enemy positions extending from Fredeburg south through Gleidorf to Schmallenburg. The reduction of this heavily defended position defeated enemy attempts to break out of the pocket. The division advanced rapidly thereafter, and with the assistance of infantry divisions quickly overcame further resistance and effected the surrender of many German divisions and two German Corps on 16 April 1945.

The outstanding success of the 7th Armored Division is the result of good training, both action, inspiring leadership and an eagerness on the part of all ranks to fight and get the job done. I am sure that a review of this operation by the military historians of the future will show that the officers and men of the 7th Armored Division did a top job. All of you should be proud. I thank you and I salute you.

I shall long wish to be associated again with the fighting 7th Armored Division

Sincerely,

J. A. VAN FLEET
Major General, U. S. Army,
Commanding

ON TO THE BALTIC

When all German restistance in Northwest Germany came to an end, the 7th Armored found itself in the big middle of its very happening, speeding the collapse with its power and aggression.

It all came about after the Division had a rest in the vicinity of Gottingen, and was working under the XVIII Corps (Airborne), only US formation committed with the British Second Army for operation north of the Elbe River. CC B, attached to the 82nd Airborne Division, was the first element to see action in this last stage battle, racing for 33 miles eastward from a bridgehead over the Elbe to the city of Ludwigslust, spearheading the Airborne Division's drive. The speed and power of the attack completely demoralized the already disorganized enemy and his garrison of 5,000 troops surrendered after offering only negligible resistance.

It was from Ludwigslust that Lt. William Knowlton took his Troop B, 87th Cavalry Reconnaissance Squadron (Mecz) to meet the Russians. The troop traveled east, spending 24 hours within the German lines, surrounded by SS units, before the Russians were contacted at 0925 on 3 May. An element of the 7th Armored made first contact with the Russians for the British Second Army.

It was also on May 3 that CC A and CC R drove north from the Elbe to reach the Baltic Sea, the first American troops to reach that body of water. In this operation, there was little need for the crushing power that the 7th had at its command. The Germans that were encountered were those surrendering — and they were numerous, very numerous. There were more than 51,000 prisoners herded into Division cages as a result of that final dash, bringing the total for nine months of combat to 113,041. Vast quantities of equipment were also taken on that day, including three airfields which were overrun — one a naval seaplane base.

And so ended the combat course that had extended from Normandy to the North German coastline.

"The Bowery Bum", famous tank of the 17th Tk Bn that fought all the way to, and into, the BALTIC Sea from the Normandy Beaches.

Announcement of V-E Day came as no great surprise to the troops of the 7th Armored. They had seen the collapse of the German Army all about them during the final days of combat. The division remained on the alert and made ready for any eventuality, and with the announcement of the official end of hostilities there was a reverent pause in memory of those comrades in arms who could not be among those present to exult in the triumph they had helped to achieve.

With weapons trained on 88,580 prisoners in Division cages, with thoughts on another war still in progress, and with eyes on the conditions about them, the gallant men of the 7th Armored Division could do little else than think of the job ahead; the magnitude had not decreased — only the nature was altered.

Officially, the war was over in Europe, and the initial combat record of the Division had been made — a glorious record that stretched for 2,260 miles over an embattled trail — a trail that led from the beaches in Normandy to the shores of the Baltic Sea.

⌒HONOR ROLL

(Winners of the Distinguished Service Cross)

Captain JACOB A. GEORGE, Jr
17th Tank Battalion (*)

Captain EDWARD J. HACKETT.
87th Cavalry Reconnaissance Squadron (Mecz) (**)

1st Lieutenant NEIL M. CHAPIN
434th Armored Field Artillery Battalion

1st Lieutenant JOHN C. CORNELL
38th Armored Infantry Battalion

1st Lieutenant MARIO J. FORTUNA
38th Armored Infantry Battalion

1st Lieutenant VINCENT E. McKENNA
434th Armored Field Artillery Battalion

1st Lieutenant DENNIS J. REGAN
440th Armored Field Artillery Battalion

2nd Lieutenant ROBERT E. MENDICK
48th Armored Infantry Battalion (**)

Corporal VICTOR P. FUNK
814th Tank Destroyer Battalion (Attached to the 7th Armored Division)·

·Technician 5th Grade GEORGE W. SCHULTZ
33rd Armored Engineer Battalion

(*) Awarded DSC as Missing in Action. Later reported Killed in Action.
(**) Posthumous Awards.

Autographs .

TEAM WORK DID IT . . .

61

CPSIA information can be obtained
at www.ICGtesting.com
Printed in the USA
LVHW081310100619
620723LV00017B/626/P